ANDALUSIA

Andalusia

Susan Thackrey

c h a x
2015

ISBN 978-0-9862640-3-0 Paperbound Edition
ISBN 978-0-9862640-4-7 Hardcover Casebound Edition

Chax Press
PO Box 162
Victoria TX 77902-0162

Publisher Acknowledgments

Chax Press would like to thank one anonymous donor, the University
of Houston-Victoria School of Arts and Sciences, and the Leslie
Scalapino–O Books Fund, for support which has made the book
possible. In addition, thank you to Amjad Nusayr for his assistance
with the Arabic typescript, and to several students, student interns,
and press assistants from the University of Houston-Victoria,
particularly Melissa Cluff, Laura Hicks, Katrina Rose, and Mareesa
Johnson, who assisted in many ways with the production of *Andalusia*.

Author Acknowledgments

I am deeply grateful to Abigail Krasner, the scholar who checked
the accuracy of my match of the Arabic to the Spanish texts, and
who also made the discovery of the missing Arabic texts in Hussein
Mu'nis' Arabic edition of the first Spanish volume of translations. Cola
Franzen's fine book of English translations from García Gómez led
me to seek out the Spanish texts. I would like to thank Luisa Franchi
and Lynn Alicia Franco for carefully reading my translations from the
Spanish. My very special thanks go to Benjamin Hollander.

Above all, I must thank all those poets, my contemporaries in living
time, now and in the past, who have informed this book.

A Note to the Reader

The poems of mine in this book, *Andalusia*, arose immediately, almost magically, in my encounter with a group of remarkable early Arabic-Andalusian poems: some arising in response to individual poems in that group, others as responses to the whole body of the early work. Startlingly, a poem of mine would sometimes come first, and I would later find its companion among the older poems.

So my own poems in this book are not translations.

They are poetry written in the presence of other poetry.

The group of early poems that touched me so deeply was discovered in 1928 by Emilio García Gómez, who first published some of them in 1930 in a small book of Spanish translations, *Poemas Arabigoandaluces*. García Gómez was a noted Spanish scholar of Arabic literature, who had found, in Cairo, a previously unknown manuscript, dated 1243, of selections from the rich tradition of Arabic-Andalusian poetry dating from the 10th to the 13th centuries. This is a tradition that interpenetrates the whole history of western lyric poetry, starting with the Troubadours, especially in its understanding of who the lover and beloved are, and of whose feelings are primary.

These early poems are the terms of engagement for me, and where a spark rose up in the presence of a particular poem I have printed that poem facing my own, in Spanish and in English. The actual translations from the Spanish are mine, and I have tried to keep them as literal as possible, in order to preserve the feeling in which my responses welled up.

It seemed important to include the original Arabic, which for the most part is from García Gómez's later publication, in 1942, of the complete Arabic manuscript, together with his complete Spanish translations, entitled *El Libro de los Campeones de ibn Sa'id al-Magribi.* Since it was "complete" it was a surprise to find that not all the poems he included in his small earlier volume are to be found in the complete edition, and so there is no Arabic text for them there. But in yet another layer to this palimpsest, the Arabic for these poems was included in a volume published in Cairo in 1957, edited by Hussein Mu'nis, an Arabic edition of García Gómez's first volume, *Poemas Arabigoandaluces,* now entitled *Al-shi'r al-Andalusi (Andalusian Poetry).*

Donne ch'avete intelletto d'amore

Dante Alighieri
Vita Nuova XIX

1

To whom
Does desire
Belong to
Lover, beloved

وددت بأن القلب شق بمديةٍ   وأدخلت فيه ثم أطبق في صدري

فأصبحت فيه لا تحلين غيره   إلى مقضي يوم القيامة والحشر

تعيشين فيه ما حييت فإن أمت   سكنت شغاف القلب في ظلم القبر

2   (50)

Quisiera Rajar Mi Corazón

Quisiera rajar mi corazón con un cuchillo, meterte
dentro y luego volver a cerrar mi pecho,

para que estuvieras en él y no habitaras en otro,
hasta el día de la resurrección y del juicio final.

Así vivirías en él mientras yo existiera y, a mi
muerte, morarías en las entretelas del corazón en la
tiniebla del sepulcro.

De Ben Hazm, de Córdoba
(994–1063)

(The numbers in parentheses over the poems in Spanish throughout this book reference García Gómez's numbering in *Poemas Arabigoandaluces*.)

I Would Like to Split My Heart

I would like to split my heart with a knife, put you
inside and then close up my heart again,

so that you would be in it and not in another,
until the day of resurrection and the last judgement.

So you would live in it while I existed, and at my
death, you would remain in the strings of my heart, in the
darkness of the grave.

2

Like a knife your
Desire splits
Your heart and in
The opening I am
Enshrined alive until
Time's end
I am a salve
A splinter
Enclosed
My mind a single
Image you in
The desert going toward
The east your heart
Opening to night and stars

ذكرت سليمى وحر الوغى ... بقلبي ساعة فارقتها

فشبهت سمر القنا قدها ... وقد ملن نحوي فعانقتها

3   *(17)*

En La Batalla

Me acordé de Sulayma cuando el ardor de la lid
era como el ardor de mi cuerpo cuando me separé
de ella.

Creí ver entre las lanzas la esbeltez de su talle y,
cuando se inclinaron hacia mí, las abracé.

> *De Abu-L-Hasan Ben Al-Qabtur-nuh,*
> *De Badajoz*

In the Battle

I remembered Sulayma when the ardor of the battle
was like the ardor of my body when I parted
from her.

I thought I saw the slimness of her body among the lances and,
when they leaned toward me, I embraced them.

3

If in the heat of
Battle your body
Burns as our bodies
Burned when we
Left one another
At dawn
What did you love
When you loved me?
If among the hundred
Slender lances of
The advancing enemy
You thought you
Saw my slender
Body and
Threw your body
Against them
What did you see
When you embraced me?

ومُهَدَّلِ الشطَّين تحسب أنه ... متساينٌ من دُرَّةٍ لصفائهِ

فاءت عليه مع الهجيرةِ سَرْحَةٌ ... صدئت لفيئتها صفيحةُ مائهِ

وتراه أزرق في غلالة سندسٍ ... كالدَّارعِ استلقى لظلِّ لوائهِ

4   *(102)*

El Río Azul

El río, de murmuradoras riberas, te haría creer,
diáfano, que es una corriente de perlas.

A mediodía le cubren de sombra los grandes árboles,
dando un color de herrumbe a la superficie del agua.

Y así lo ves, azul, envuelto en su túnica de brocado,
como un guerrero con loriga tendido a la sombra
de su bandera.

> *De Muhammad Ben Galib Al-*
> *Rusafi, de la Ruzafa de Valencia*
> *(m. 1177)*

The Blue River

The river of murmuring banks, diaphanous,
could make you believe that it is a stream of pearls.

At mid-day the great trees cover it with shadow,
giving a color of rust to the surface of the water.

And so you see it, blue, wrapped in its tunic of brocade,
like a warrior in armor, stretched out in the shadow
of his banner.

4

A warrior sees
The tree-shadowed blue
River as a warrior who
Is lying stretched
Out not in
Death but
In sleep at
Mid-day under
A banner patterning
His armor with
Shadow and light he
Never sees

As for myself
I kneel by
The side of that
Running stream
Yearning to see my
Reflection as
God yearns trying
To imagine my face

5

My sadness resides
At the source
Of the river small
Reeds in the
Rocky spring

أتيتني وهلال الجو   مطلع   قبيل قرع النصارى   للنواقيس

كحاجب الشيخ عم الشيب   أكثره   وأخمص الرجل في لطفٍ وتقويس

ولاح في الأفق قوس الله   مكتسباً   من كل لونٍ كأذناب   الطواويس

6   *(49)*

La Visita De La Amada

*Viniste a mí un poco antes de que los cristianos
tocasen las campanas, cuando la media luna surgía
en el cielo,*

*como la ceja de un anciano cubierta casi del todo
por las canas, o como la delicada curva de la planta
del pie.*

*Y, aunque era aún de noche, con tu venida brilló
en el horizonte el arco del Señor, vestido de todos los
colores, como la cola de los pavones.*

*De Ben Hazm, de Córdoba
(994-1063)*

The Visit of the Beloved

You came to me a little before the Christians
rang their bells, when the half moon rose
in the sky,

Like the eyebrow of an old man covered almost completely
with white hair, or like the delicate curve of the sole
of the foot.

And although it was still night, with your coming
the rainbow shone on the horizon, clothed in every
color, like the peacock's tail.

6

Old poet your
Eyebrows danced
With your eyes'
Delight when I
Arrived with the
Half-moon and the
Christians' bells but
Which of the
Christians' three
Night bells rang and
Was the moon
Growing or
Falling from
The full?
Perhaps
Only my
Heart leaps
In the dark seeing
The equal
Beauty of the old
Half-moon

هم نظروا لواحظها فهاموا ... وتشرب لب شاربها المدام

يخاف الناس مقلتها سواها ... أيذعر قلب حامله الحسام

سما طرفي إليها وهو باك ... وتحت الشمس ينسكب الغمام

وأذكر قدها فأنوح وجدا ... على الأغصان تنتدب الحمام

وأعقب بينها في الصدر غما ... إذا غربت ذكاء أتى الظلام

7   (69)

La Amada

Cuantos miran sus ojos, quedan prendados; que el
vino bebe la razón del que lo bebe.

Todos temen su mirada, menos ella, pues ¿acaso
hace temblar la espada el corazón del que la empuña?

Alzóse hacia ella mi vista, mientras lloraba, y
vio desatarse las nubes bajo el sol de su frente.

Recordando su talle, gimo de amor, como las palomas
que lloran sobre las ramas.

Su separación ha dejado en mi pecho una negra
tristeza, como las tinieblas vienen cuando se pone
el sol.

> *Del alfaquí cordobés Umar Ben Umar,*
> *Qadi de Córdoba y Sevilla en tiempo*
> *de los Almohades*

The Beloved

All those who gaze into her eyes are captured: as
wine drinks up the reason of those who drink it.

All fear her glance, except herself—does the heart of
the one who grips the sword cause it to tremble?

I raised my eyes up toward her, while I was weeping, and
saw the clouds break up under the sunshine of her countenance.

Remembering her waist, I moan with love, like
the doves that cry on the branches.

Her going has left a black sorrow in my breast,
like the shadows that come when the sun sets.

7

If I am your
Beloved why am
I your enemy how
Can my glances
Without feeling cut
You to the heart you
Are a warrior you
Know in the
Desire of battle the cold
Sword does not
Tremble but the
Heart of the warrior
Trembles with the
Pulse of
Passion or
Compassion
My eyes
Light on you like a
Butterfly alights upon a
Crimson flower in
This garden
When night blinds
My eyes I make my
Way by your sweet
Fragrance rising on the
Cool night air

يفدي الصحيفة ناظري فبياضها ... ببياضه سوادها بسواد

8   (10)

La Lectura

Mi pupila rescata lo que está preso en la página:
lo blanco a lo blanco y lo negro a lo negro.

Del célebre Ben Ammar de
Silves, visir de Mutamid de Sevilla
(m. 1086)

Reading

The pupil of my eye rescues what has been captured in the page:
the white rescues the white, and the black the black.

8

I am
Illiterate
At night the
Stars enter
My eyes

أقلب طرفي في السماء ترددا ... لعلي أرى النجم الذي أنت تنظر

وأستعرض الركبان من كل وجهة ... لعلي بمن قد شم عرفك أظفر

وأستقبل الأرواح عند هبوبها ... لعل نسيم الريح عنك يخبر

وأمشي وما لي في الطريق مآرب ... عسى نغمة باسم الحبيب ستذكر

وألمح من ألقاه من غير حاجة ... عسى لمحة من نور وجهك تسفر

Ausencia

Sin cesar recorro con mis ojos los cielos, por si
viese la estrella que tú estás contemplando.

Pregunto a los viajeros de todas las tierras, por
si encontrara alguno que hubiese aspirado tu fragrancia.

Cuando los vientos soplan, hago que me den en el
rostro, por si la brisa me trajese tus nuevas.

Voy errante por los caminos, sin meta ni rumbo:
tal vez una canción me recuerde tu nombre.

Miro furtivamente, sin necesidad, a cuantos me
encuentro, por si atisbara un rasgo de tu hermosura.

De Abu Bakr Al-Turtusi
(1059-1126)

9

Absence

Ceaselessly I search the heavens with my eyes, so that
perhaps I might see the star that you are contemplating.

I question travelers from every land, so that perhaps
I might encounter someone who has breathed in
your fragrance.

When the winds blow, I make certain they blow
in my face, so that perhaps the breeze might carry news of you to me.

I wander on the roads, without goal or direction:
perhaps a song will awaken your name.

I watch secretly, without necessity, all those I meet,
so that perhaps I might spy one feature of your beauty.

9

The words of your song
Reach me one after
The other as a running
Stream a slight
Wind or a stranger
Might carry an
Odor a rustle a
Gleam of me to
You I
Long as
You long trying
To find the smallest hint
Of your perfection
Suddenly present
How can we ever meet?
I am not a
Fixed star I too
Wander looking

خضبت بنان مديرها بشعاعها ... فعل العرارة في شفاه الربرب

10   *(2)*

El Reflejo del Vino

El reflejo del vino atravesado por la luz colorea
de rojo los dedos del copero, como el enebro deja
teñido el hocico del antílope.

> *De Abu-l-Hasan Ali Ben Hisn,*
> *Secretario de Mutadid de Sevilla.*
> *(Siglo xi)*

The Reflection of Wine

The reflection of wine pierced by the light stains
the fingers of the cupbearer red, as the juniper
dyes the muzzle of the antelope.

10

As impossible in
This light-filled
Garden for you to
Taste the red
Reflections of the
Wine upon my
Fingers as for
Me to see
The red juice of the
Fruit staining
My mouth

الريح أقود ما يكون لأنها ... تبدي خفايا الردف والأعكان

11 *(76)*

El Viento

*No hay mayor alcahuete que el viento, pues levanta
los vestidos y descubre las partes ocultas del cuerpo,*

*Y ablanda la resistencia de las ramas, haciendo
que se inclinen a besar la faz de los estanques.*

*Por eso los amantes lo emplean como tercero que
lleva mensajes a sus amigos y enamorados.*

De Ben Said Al-Magribi
(1214-1274)

The Wind

There is no better procurer than the wind, since
it lifts up clothing and uncovers the hidden parts of the
body.

And softens the resistance of the branches, making
them bend to kiss the face of the pool.

For this reason lovers use it as a go-between to
carry messages to their intimate friends and to those who
have enamoured them.

11

The wind is stirred by
The wings of
Birds flying
Through still air
The branches weighted
Where they sit and
Sing the words of their
Song moving the
Air between them even
More delicately than
The feathers of their
Wings as most
Lightly the
Breath passes
From lover to
Lover like summer
Breeze unveiling each
To each

بعثت بمرآة إليك بديعة ... فأطلع بسامي أفقها قمر السعد

لننظر فيها حسن وجهك منصفا ... وتعذرني فيما أكن من الوجد

فأرسل بذاك الخد لحظك برهة ... لتجني منه ما جناه من الورد

مثالك فيها منك أقرب ملمسا ... وأكثر إحسانا وأبقى على العهد

12   (33)

Regalando Un Espejo

Te envío un espejo precioso: haz surgir en su alto
horizonte tu rostro, luna de buen agüero.

Así apreciarás con justeza tu hermosura y disculparás
la pasión que me consume.

¡Ay, con ser furtiva, tu imagen es más accesible
que tú, mas benévola y mejor cumplidora de promesas!

Del poeta sevillano Ben Al-Sabuni
(Siglo xiii)

The Gift of a Mirror

I send you a beautiful mirror: let your countenance appear
on its far horizon, a moon of good omen.

So you will justly appreciate your own beauty and pardon
the passion that consumes me.

Oh, despite its furtive being, your image is more accessible
than you, more benevolent, and a better fulfiller of promises!

12

Thank you for
Your gift of
A most beautiful
Mirror I have
Looked but I
Cannot see what
You said you
Wanted me to see
The serene face
Of the most
Beautiful
Moon rising over
Its horizon I see
My own
Face weeping
Because I cannot
Give you
What I do
Not own

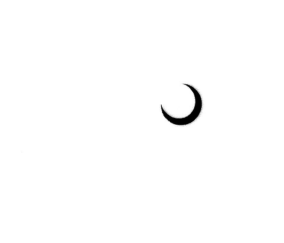

13

I was never
Beautiful still I
Loved you
Summoned like
A sun to
Burn alone
Toward death

14

You say you came
To God through
Me my beloved
Body the ladder you
Climbed
To heaven

Desert is
Earth without
Water my body's
Bones these
Grains of sand

أقبل في حلة موردة ... كالبدر في حلة من الشفق

تحسبه كلما أراق دمي ... يمسح في ثوبه ظبى الحدق

15   (32)

La Túnica Roja

Su blanca figura avanzó cubierta con un vestido
del color de la rosa, como la luna envuelta en el
manto del crepúsculo.

Diríase que, cuantas veces han derramado mi sangre
los arpones de sus ojos, los ha enjugado después
en el vistido.

Del poeta sevillano Ben Al-Sabuni
(Siglo xiii)

The Red Tunic

*Her white form advances dressed in clothing
the color of roses, like the moon enfolded in the
mantle of twilight.*

*You could say that each time the spears of her eyes
have spilled my blood, she has dried them afterward
on her clothing.*

15

Layla

Looking for you I
Found you and
Stood before
You dressed in a
Crimson robe my
Hands stained red
With henna you
Paused drinking in the
Beauty of this
Image and
Went on looking
For me my
Grief thirst
In the desert

Looking for you I
Rose from the red
Dust of my tomb
Again and again

ومعاقل من سوسن قد شيدت ... أيدي الربيع بناءها فوق العذب

شرفاتها من فضة وحماتها ... حول الأمير لهم سيوف من ذهب

16   *(44)*

La Azucena

*Las manos de la primavera han amurallado, encima
de los tallos, los castillos de la azucena;*

*Castillos con almenas de plata y donde los defensores,
agrupados en torno del príncipe, tienen espadas de oro.*

> *De Ben Darrach Al-Qastalli,
> Probablemente de Qastalla en el
> Algarve; pero que vivió en Córdoba
> (958-1030)*

The Lily

The hands of spring have built the castle walls of the lilies upon their stalks;

Castles with parapets of silver, where the defenders, clustered around the prince, hold swords of gold.

16

What warrior so
Battle-hardened he
Would see this
Lily as a silver
Castle built
By spring within
Whose battlements the
Knights with
Golden Swords
Erect protect
Their prince–
Warrior look
This is my silver
Cup overflowing at
The lip where
You might
Drink these are
Not golden
Swords they
Are my
Tongues whose words
Of longing pour
Unguarded
Into the
Spring air

ولما وقفنا غداة النوى وقد أسقط البين ما في يدي

رأيت الهوادج فيها البدور ... عليها البراقع من عسجد

وتحت البراقع مقلوبها ... تدب على ورد خد ندي

تسالم من وطئت خده ... وتلدغ قلب الشجي المكمد

17   (5)

Despedida

*Cuando en la mañana que se fueron nos despedimos,
llenos de tristeza por la próxima ausencia,*

*Vi a lomos de los camellos los palanquines en que
se iban, bellas como lunas, cubiertas por sus velos
de oro.*

*Bajo los velos reptaban los escorpiones de los aladares
sobre las rosas de la mejilla fragante.*

*Son escorpiones que no dañan la mejilla que huellan,
y, en cambio, pican el corazón del triste enamorado.*

*De Ben Chaj, de Badajoz
(Siglo XI)*

The Farewell

When, on the morning that they left we said
farewell, full of sadness for the coming absence,

I saw on the backs of the camels the
palanquins they travelled in—they who were as beautiful
as moons, covered by golden veils.

Beneath the veils the scorpions of their tears
crept over the roses of their fragrant cheeks.

They are scorpions that do not injure the cheek which
they mark—instead, they sting the heart of the sad
lover.

17

How do you
Know the heart of
The moon perhaps
There is one
Kind of
Time always restoring
Her bright
Face to perfect
Bloom another
Eating
Her fragrant heart
In grief

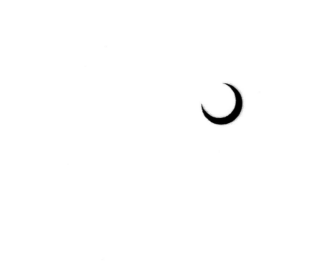

18

No man has
Desired me except
For my
Compassion I have
No word to
Speak at death to
Open heaven

الروض مخضر الربى متجمل ... للناظرين بأجمل الألوان

وكأنما بسطت هناك سوارها ... خود زهت بقلائد العقيان

وكأنما فتقت هناك نوافح ... من مسكة عجنت بعرف البان

والطير يسجع في الغصون كأنما ... تقرأ القيان فيه على العيدان

والماء مطرد يسيل عبابه ... كسلاسل من فضة وجمان

بهجات حسن أكملت فكأنها ... حسن اليقين وبهجة الإيمان

19   (60)

Un Jardín

*El jardín de verdes altozanos se adorna para los
espectadores con el color más bello,*

*Como si hubiese expuesto en él su ajuar una doncella
resplandeciente con sus collares de oro,*

*O se hubiesen vertido allí cazoletas de almizcle
amasado con ban purísimo.*

*Los pájaros gorjean en los ramos, como si fuesen
cantoras inclinadas sobre los laúdes.*

*El agua continua deja caer sus caños como cadenillas
de plata y de perlas.*

*Son esplendores de hermosura tan perfectos, que
parecen la belleza de la certidumbre o el brillo
de la fe.*

*De Abd Allah Ben Simak,
de Granada (m. 1145)*

A Garden

The garden of small green hills adorns itself for
its admirers with the most beautiful colors,

As if in it the dowry of a maiden were being displayed
shining with its necklaces of gold,

Or bowls of musk mixed with the purest incense
were being poured out there.

The birds warble on the branches, as if they were
singers bending over their lutes.

The water continues to let fall its streams like
chains of silver and pearls.

They are splendors of a loveliness so perfect, that
they are like the beauty of certainty or the brilliance of faith.

19

I too love the
Greenness of
The garden but
Unlike you in
My love I
Become as she
Is dressing in
Perfumed colors like
A bride wearing
Her dowry as
If it were brilliant
Gold glittering as I
Bend over the
Lute whose sounds
Shine like drops
Of water falling one
By one into this
Song like her my
Love is not
Consumed in the perfect
Certainty of
The marriage room or
In the radiant
Ascent to heaven

لئن كان البياض لباس حزنٍ ... بأندلس فذاك من الصواب

ألم ترني لبست بياض شيبي ... لأني قد حزنت على الشباب

20   (81)

El Luto En Al-Andalus

Si es el blanco el color de los vestidos de luto en
al-Andalus, cosa justa es.

¿No me ves a mí, que me he vestido con el blanco
de las canas, porque estoy de luto por la juventud?

De Abu-L-Hasan Al-Husri,
"el Ciego" (m. 1095)

Mourning in Al-Andalus

*If white is the color of mourning clothes in
al-Andalus, it is a just thing.*

*Don't you see me, who has dressed myself in the whiteness
of my white hair, because I am in mourning for my youth?*

20

Alba

In al-Andalus
It is our
Custom to wear
White in
Mourning remembering
The white
Dawn when lover
Was parted from
Her beloved your
White hair old
Poet is not
Worn in
Mourning for
Your youth but
Revelation of the
Secret of our
Brightening embrace

غصن يهتز في دعص نقا ... يجتني منه فؤادي حرقا

سال لام الصدغ في صفحته ... سيلان التبر وافى الورقا

فتناهى الحسن فيه إنما ... يحسن الغصن إذا ما أورقا

أصبحت شمسا وفوه مغربا ... ويد الساقي المحيي مشرقا

فإذا ما غربت في فمه ... تركت في الخد منه شفقا

21   (41)

La Hermosa En La Orgía

Su talle flexible era una rama que se balanceaba
sobre el montón de arena de su cadera y de la que
cogía mi corazón frutos de fuego.

Los rubios cabellos que asomaban por sus sienes
dibujaban un lam en la blanca página de su mejilla,
como oro que corre sobre plata.

Estaba en el apogeo de su belleza, como la rama
cuando se viste de hojas.

El vaso lleno de rojo néctar era, entre sus dedos
blancos, como un crepúsculo que amaneció encima
de una aurora.

Salía el sol del vino, y era su boca el poniente, y
el oriente la mano del copero, que al escanciar
pronunciaba fórmulas corteses.

Y, al ponerse en el delicioso ocaso de sus labios,
dejaba el crepúsculo en su mejilla.

> *Del príncipe omeya Marwan Ben*
> *Abd Al-Rahman, llamado*
> *Al-Taliq, ("el Amnistiado")*
> *(m. 1009)*

21

The Beauty at the Revelry

Her supple waist was a branch that swayed
over the sand-dunes of her hips, and
from it my heart picked fruits of fire.

The blonde hair which showed at her temples
drew the letter "lam" on the white page of her
cheek, like gold that flows over silver.

She was at the peak of her beauty, like a branch
when it is clothed in leaves.

The glass full of red nectar between her white fingers,
was like a twilight appearing over a dawn.

The sun arose from the wine, and her mouth was the setting
sun, and the hand of the cupbearer like the east, and while serving
the wine he spoke courtly words.

And, upon going down in the delicious sunset of her lips,
the sun left a faint light upon her cheek.

21

I am the dancer with
Willow waist
Swaying as I
Accept the cup of
Wine like the
Rising sun that
Sets in my
Mouth as I
Drink lighting my
Cheeks at dusk with
Dawn the poem ends
Here I want
It to follow the
Sun through the
Gates of
Dark journeying
In the night to
Ignite one by
One the
Fires at the
Root of my
Tongue of
My heart of my
Belly the
Place this
Poem begins

22

The young deer
Stands in an open
Field where the grass has
Dried up like
The milk of her
Mother gone with
The first winds of
Sunrise to answer
The scent of
Love again

وطائعة الوصال عففت عنها ... وما الشيطان فيها بالمطاع

بدت في الليل سافرة فباتت ... دياجي الليل سافرة القناع

وما من لحظة إلا وفيها ... إلى فتن القلوب لها دواعي

فملكت الهوى جمحات شوقي ... لأجري في العفاف على طباعي

وبت بها مبيت الطفل يظما ... فيمنعه الفطام عن الرضاع

كذاك الروض ما فيه لمثلي ... سوى نظر وشم من متاع

ولست من السوائم مهملات ... فأتخذ الرياض من المراعي

23   (39)

Castidad

Aunque estaba pronta a entregarse, me abstuve de
ella, y no obedecí la tentación que me ofrecía Satán.

Apareció sin velo en la noche, y las tinieblas
nocturnas, iluminadas por su rostro, también levantaron
aquella vez sus velos.

No había mirada suya en la que no hubiera
incentivos que revolucionaban los corazones.

Mas di fuerzas al precepto divino que condena la
lujuria sobre las arrancadas caprichosas del corcel
de mi pasión, para que mi instinto no se rebelase
contra la castidad.

Y así, pasé con ella la noche como el pequeño
camello sediento al que el bozal impide mamar.

Tal, un vergel, donde para uno como yo no hay
otro provecho que el ver y el oler.

Que no soy yo como las bestias abandonadas que
toman los jardines como pasto.

> *De Ben Farach, de Jaén, Autor del*
> *Libro de los Huertos*
> *(m. 976)*

23

Chastity

Although she was ready to surrender, I abstained
from her, and did not yield to the temptation Satan offered me.

She appeared unveiled in the night, and the shadows of the night,
illuminated by her face, raised their veils at that moment.

There is no glance of hers that could not make
hearts turn.

But I gave more strength to the divine precept, which condemns
lust, over the capricious and sudden starts of the horses
of my passion, so that my instinct did not revolt
against chastity.

And so I passed the night with her like a little
thirsty camel, that a muzzle keeps from nursing.

Such a one as she is an orchard, where for one like me
there is no other benefit than sight and fragrance.

I am not like those abandoned animals that
take gardens for pastures.

23

When I came to
You unveiled
In the evening you
Turned to praise
The ways you misunderstood
My love giving your
Own name to
My desire
What I give does
Not deplete
Me my
Virtue cannot be
Returned to
Me by you as if
I were your
Enemy and you
Refused to take my
Life would you halter
A gazelle would you
Shroud the desert from
Spring rain?

Walk
With me in
This garden graze
With me
In this
Green field

ومطبقة لفقن احسن ما ترى   كما انطبق الجفنان يوما على الكرى

اذا فتحها مديه فلت مقلة   احدبها فتح العيون لتنطرا

وباطنها من باطن الاذن خلقة   غصونا اذا شبهتها وتكسرا

24   (4)

La Nuez

Es una envoltura formada por dos piezas tan unidas,
que es lindo de ver: parecen los párpados cuando
se cierran en el sueño.

Si la hiende un cuchillo, dirías que es una pupila
a la que pone convexa el esfuerzo de mirar.

Y su interior podrías compararlo al de la oreja,
por sus repliegues y escondrijos.

> *De Abu Bakr Muhammad Ben*
> *Al-Qutiyya, cortesano de Mutadid*
> *De Sevilla*

The Walnut

It is a covering formed of two pieces joined together
so that it is beautiful to see: they look like eyelids when
they are closed in sleep.

If a knife splits it, you would say it is the pupil of an eye,
whose effort to see pushes it into a convex shape.

And you could compare the inside to an ear,
because of its convolutions and crannies.

24

Eyelid

Cleave what was
Closed in sleep
Reveal the waking
Sense leave me
To rise to
Dress in the crimson
Petals scattered
Across the floor

يا أيها الملك الذي آباؤه شم الأنوف من الطراز الأول

حليت بالنعم الجسام جسيمة عنقي فحل يدي كذاك بأجدل

وامنن به ضافي الجناح كأنما حذيت قوائمه بريح شمأل

متلفتاً والطل ينثر برده منه على مثل اليماني المحمل

أغدو به عجباً أصرف في يدي ريحاً وآخذ مطلقاً بمكبل

25   *(15)*

Petición De Un Halcón

¡Oh rey, cuyos padres fueron altaneros y del más
egregio rango!

Tú, que adornaste mi cuello con el collar de tus
favores, grandes como perlas y engarzados como las
perlas en el hilo, adorna ahora mi mano con un halcón.

Hónrame con uno de límpidas alas, cuyo plumaje
se haya combado por el viento del Norte.

¡Con qué orgullo saldré con él al alba, jugando
mi mano con el viento, para apresar lo libre con lo
encadenado!

De Abd Al-Aziz Ben al-Qab-Turnuh
Secretario de Mutawakkil de Badajoz
(muerto después de 1126)

Petition for a Falcon

Oh king, whose fathers were soaring birds of
the highest rank!

You, who have adorned my neck with the necklace of your
favors, as large as pearls and threaded like
pearls on a string, adorn now my hand with a falcon.

Honor me with one with clean wings, whose feathers
have been bent by the north wind.

With what pride I will go out with it at dawn, matching
my hand against the wind, in order to capture the free with
the enchained.

25

As the smallest bird of
The air I have died
Ten thousand times
Pierced by the golden
Talons of those birds who
Are slaves of the king my
Blood like rain in
The dawn
I am your
Beloved uninjured I
Appear in the light of
The morning and evening my
Feathers grow out of
The wind if finally
You ask me to
Come to you no
One will envy you your
Prize if I
Fly I will not
Return at your
Demand but at my
Heart's no blood
Will stain your glove

كأننـا لـم نَبِت والوصـل ثالثنـا والسعد قد غَضَّ من أجفان واشينـا

سِرّانِ في خاطرِ الظَّلْمـاء يَكتُمُنـا حتى يكـاد لسـان الصبـح يُفشينـا

Fragmentos De La "Qasida En Nun"

Alejados uno de otro, mis costados están secos de
pasión por ti, y en cambio no cesan mis lágrimas...

Al perderte, mis días han cambiado y se han tornado
negros, cuando contigo hasta mis noches eran blancas...

Diríase que no hemos pasado juntos la noche, sin
más tercero que nuestra propia unión, mientras
nuestra buena estrella hacía bajar los ojos de nuestros censores:

Éramos dos secretos en el corazón de las tinieblas,
hasta que la lengua de la aurora estaba a punto de
denunciarnos.

De Ben Zaydun, de Córdoba
(1003-1070)

26

Fragments of the "Qasida en Nun"

Parted from one another, my body dried up with
passion for you, and in exchange my tears never ceased...

Losing you, my days have changed and have turned
black, while with you even my nights were white...

One might say that we never passed the night together, without
any mediator except our own union, while
our good star closed the eyes of our critics...

We were two secrets in the heart of the darkness,
until the tongue of dawn was just on the point of
denouncing us.

26

It tears at my heart
And my eyes
Remembering
How we two lay
As a single egg
In the nest of the night
Her heartbeat completely
Surrounding us one
Star our guardian we
Were her secret until
Day shattered it
And we parted into
The light delivered
Into the eyes of the
Jealous world named
By the tongue
Of time

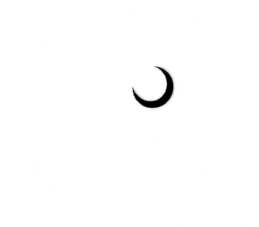

27

What has been
Called sacred
Is the secret
Door into the
Shaded garden if
You love
Me you
Must love what
I am a
Stone in the dusty
Road

والبدر كالمرآة غير صقلها ... عبث الغواني فيه بالأنفاس

والليل متلبس بضوء صباهة . . . التباس النقس بالقرطاس

La Luna

*La luna es como un espejo cuyo alinde ha sido
empañado por los suspiros de las doncellas.*

*Y la noche se viste con la luz de su lámpara como
la negra tinta se viste con el blanco papel.*

> *Del secretario cordobés Ben Burd
> El Nieto (m. 1053)*

.

The Moon

*The moon is like a mirror whose quicksilver has been
misted over by the sighs of young girls.*

*And the night is clothed with the light of her lamp like
the black ink is clothed by the white paper.*

28

Look how
My illusions
Illuminate
My night

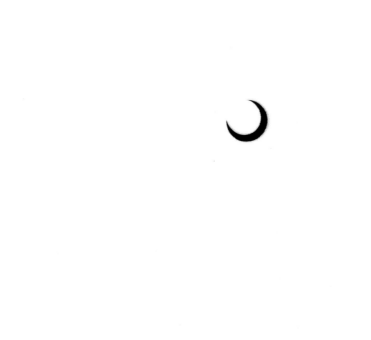

29

Where object
Touches
Mirror image
Disappears

About the Author

Susan Thackrey, a poet who lives and works in San Francisco, began to compose poetry at the age of three. She was an inaugurating student in the Poetics Program at New College in San Francisco in 1980, and studied with Robert Duncan and Diane di Prima formally and informally over a number of years. Thackrey has given invitational lectures on Robert Duncan, Charles Olson, and George Oppen, including as a keynote speaker at the George Oppen Conference in Buffalo, and most recently on Duncan's *The H.D. Book* for the San Francisco Poetry Center. Since reading Homer in Greek over a five year period with Robert Duncan and some of her poet contemporaries, an important and lively part of her life in poetry has almost always included variously focused and long-lived reading groups with other poets.

Her day jobs have included co-founding and managing the art gallery Thackrey and Robertson in San Francisco, as well as her current work as a Jungian analyst in the C.G. Jung Institute of San Francisco. There she has taught, spoken, and published, focusing especially on art, recently publishing a talk and essay on Jung's paintings for *The Red Book: Reflections on C.G. Jung's Liber Novus* (Routledge).

Her poems have appeared in a number of journals, including *Five Fingers, Hambone, Talisman, Traverse,* and *Volt.* Current books in print, in addition to *Andalusia*, are *Empty Gate* (Listening Chamber), and *George Oppen: A Radical Practice* (O Books and The San Francisco Poetry Center).

About Chax

Founded in 1984 in Tucson, Arizona, Chax has published nearly 200 books in a variety of formats, including hand printed letterpress books and chapbooks, hybrid chapbooks, book arts editions, and trade paperback editions such as the book you are holding. In August 2014 Chax moved to Victoria, Texas, and is presently located in the University of Houston-Victoria Center for the Arts, which has generously supported the publication of *Andalusia*, which has also received support from an anonymous donor and from the Leslie Scalapino–O Books Fund. Chax is an independent 501(c)(3) organization which depends on support from various government and private funders, and, primarily, from individual donors and readers.

Chax Press has had a helpful and brilliant Board of Directors over the course of our history, with members including Ron Silliman, Marjorie Perloff, Elizabeth Robinson, Jeanne Heuving, Karen Brennan, Cynthia Hogue, and more. Current board members are Lidia Serrata, James Higgins, Charles Alexander, Cynthia Miller, Joshua Metlyng, Mridul Nanda (President), and Ken Bacher.

Recent and current books-in-progress include *The Complete Light Poems*, by Jackson Mac Low, *Life–list*, by Jessica Smith, *Diesel Hand*, by Nico Vassilakis, *Dark Ladies*, by Steve McCaffery, and *Leaves of Class*, by Kit Robinson.

You may find CHAX online at http://chax.org